The First People in the World

SHAKE HANDS with a chimpanzee, and what will he do? He will study you and examine your hand, for he is just as curious about you as you are about him.

It's no wonder that apes look and act almost like people. Apes and people are relatives. They belong to the same big family—the creatures with hands.

Scientists have tried to learn the history of the whole family. They have found that some branches of the family appeared in the world long ago. Later came the apes, and finally people.

Who, or what, were the ancestors of man? And how did the first people get their start in the world? The scientists have worked hard to answer these questions. They have dug up fossil bones of many of the creatures with hands. They have discovered bones of a few early people, and also some rough stone tools.

From these traces of the past, the scientists have pieced together a wonderful story. It is the story of the first people, and how they came to be.

Many millions of years ago there were neither apes nor people in the world. There were no cats nor dogs, no horses nor cows. Giant reptiles ruled the land.

The reptiles laid eggs, which were left to hatch by themselves. The young pecked their way out of the eggs. Then they went looking for food. Some starved. Others were eaten by larger animals. Out of a batch of reptile eggs, very few of the young ones lived to grow up.

Creatures of an entirely different kind lived in the trees. They were tiny, furry things that hunted insects. The mother had milk glands, and nursed her young.

These creatures were the first milk-feeders, or mammals.

Baby mammals had a better start in life than baby reptiles. Before birth, they were carried inside their mother's body. There they were snug and safe. After birth, their mother kept them in a nest.

Because they were fed with nourishing milk, young insect-eaters grew quickly. Soon after birth, they were big enough to leave the nest. They followed their mother, and went out into the great, green world of the trees. They watched their mother chasing insects. They tried to do it, too. Gradually, they learned how to catch their own food.

The dinosaurs began to die out, and finally none were left. Then it was safe for insect-eaters to come down from the trees. Many made their homes on the ground.

Insect-eaters lived and died, and young ones took the place of the old. The young were always a little different from their parents. As time went on, little differences added up and made big differences. In this way, new kinds of mammals arose.

Some of the mammals stayed in the trees. Among them was a remarkable creature, the lemur. The lemur had no feet—instead, he had four hands. And how well he used them! He could grasp a branch tightly, crooking his fingers around one side of the branch and his thumb around the other side. And he was able to pick fruit and steal birds' eggs.

Among some of the lemurs, the snout became shorter and shorter. From these lemurs came creatures that had no snout at all. They had monkey faces, for they were the first monkeys.

A modern monkey, as you can plainly see, has no snout. His face is flat, and his eyes are set in front. Both eyes look straight ahead. Both see the same thing, and see it sharp and clear. That is good for a creature living in the treetops. A monkey can tell just how far away a branch is. So he dares to jump. He goes jumping from branch to branch and from tree to tree.

When you visit a zoo, watch a young monkey and notice how he investigates everything. He doesn't go around sniffing at things, as a dog does. Instead, he handles things with his nimble fingers, and examines them with his keen eyes. That's how a monkey learns.

Monkeys of one kind gradually became larger. Their chests became broader, and their arms longer. Their tails grew shorter, then disappeared. These big, tailless creatures were the first apes.

The apes were too heavy to run and jump through the trees. But they could reach out with their long arms and swing from bough to bough. Some of them became very expert swingers. These apes had especially long arms. Their fingers were long, too—all except the thumbs. When they crooked their fingers around a branch, their thumbs stuck out underneath. The thumb was useless. In time, it became smaller and smaller.

Today there are four kinds of apes—the chimpanzee, the orang-utan, the gibbon, and the gorilla. All have the expert swinger's hand. They have long, strong fingers and a tiny, weak thumb.

The chimpanzee swings pretty well. The orang-utan, which has longer arms, swings farther and better. But the gibbon, the smallest ape, is the champion acrobat of the world. He has enormously long arms. He grasps a branch and takes a mighty swing. Then he lets go and shoots through the air, straight to the spot he is aiming for.

The huge gorilla has problems. When full-grown, he can hardly climb at all. He is much too heavy for swinging through the trees. So he has to spend his life on the ground.

But the gorilla is a misfit on the ground, too. His legs are short, and his feet are like hands. He must use his arms as crutches, propping himself on his knuckles as he lumbers along.

The poor gorilla! He isn't a good swinger. He isn't a good runner. He is much too big and clumsy. He doesn't seem to belong anywhere. There are few gorillas left in the world. Some day the last of them will be gone.

Insect-eater, lemur, monkey, ape—one after another they came. Some of these creatures were small; others were large. Some had tails; others had none. But the biggest difference was in their brains.

The brain of the insect-eater was small and simple. The lemur's brain was larger and more complicated. The monkey had a still larger and better brain. The ape had the best brain of all.

The better its brain, the more slowly an animal grows. Scientists have found this out by studying baby lemurs, monkeys, and apes. Even before they are born, these animals grow at different rates, some faster, some slower. An unborn lemur spends four months inside its mother's body. An unborn monkey is carried by its mother for five months. An unborn chimpanzee is carried for eight months.

After birth, too, the creature with the better brain needs more time to develop. A baby lemur walks in a few days, and is grown-up in a year. A monkey walks in a month, and is grown-up in three years. A baby chimpanzee is almost as helpless as a human baby. It can't walk until it is six months old. And it takes eight years to grow up.

As a rule, the creatures with hands live in groups. Monkeys travel in large bands, and seem to like one another's company. They chatter all the time. Often they are hidden from one another by leaves and branches. But they chatter and chatter, and each monkey hears the others. He knows where the band is, so he doesn't get lost.

In a band of chimpanzees, there are several mothers and babies, young apes of different ages, and grown-up males. It is good that they all like to live together. The young have playmates, and the babies have grown-ups to protect them. If a leopard comes prowling through the forest, some watchful member of the band will see him and cry out. Quickly, all take to the trees.

In a band of gibbons, many voices are heard, making different kinds of sounds. These sounds are not words. They are chuckles, wails, screams, or groans. They tell about feelings. When gibbons chuckle, it means that everything is all right, so the band goes on feeding. But if one of them gives a cry of fear, the whole band is ready to flee. By hearing one another's voices, they know one another's feelings. Then they act together.

For millions of years, apes have been living in bands. If they hadn't stayed together, the young could never have grown up. They would have been killed by enemies, and there would be no apes in the world today.

Long ago, different branches of the ape family lived in different parts of the forest. Some stayed in the center, where the trees grew thickest. These apes were the ones who became expert swingers. Others lived at the edge of the forest, near grassy meadows. These apes spent most of their time on the ground. There they found plenty of food. They dug up roots and grubs, and pulled small animals from their holes. In order to see over the tall grass, they walked upright.

The apes of the ground had an old-fashioned type of hand. Their thumbs were big and strong, like a lemur's. Because of this, they could hold things between thumb and fingertips.

The swinger's type of thumb made it harder to handle things. Suppose your thumb were tiny and useless. Pick up a pencil with your fingers alone, and try to write without using your thumb. It's hard, isn't it? Then hold the pencil in the usual way, between your thumb and fingertips. What a difference!

The hands of the ground apes were like yours. They could pick up sticks or stones, handle them easily, and use them as weapons. Often, weapons were needed. Fierce wild dogs roved about. If they tried to sneak up on a young ape, the whole band would grab sticks and stones and drive the dogs away.

Can we really be sure how the ground apes lived? It doesn't help very much to study chimpanzees or other apes of today. They are all swingers. There are no creatures like the ancient ground apes. So we must use our imagination and try to guess how they lived.

Probably the ground apes used pointed sticks to dig up roots, crayfish, and clams. If so, how did they sharpen the sticks? Perhaps they would smash stones, one after another, until they managed to get some sharp pieces. With these, they would sharpen the sticks.

Eventually, they found a way to make better digging-sticks. Perhaps this is what happened.

The ground apes lived in a land where there were many volcanoes. When a volcano started to erupt, the apes were terrified. They saw enormous dark clouds billowing over their heads. And streams of hot lava pouring down the slope. And trees flaming up like torches. All creatures ran from the fiery mountain, and the ground apes ran with the rest.

Trees were burned, yet sticks could still be found. The sticks had been scorched by the heat, which made the wood hard. The ground apes were glad to discover this. They began to use scorched wood for their digging-sticks.

After a while, the ground apes had another idea.
They looked for a fire, or a heap of embers. When they
found one, they held their sticks in the heat, to make the
points hard.

Every day the ground apes did several different kinds of work. After finishing one task, they had to decide where they would go next, and what they would do. Look for fire, hunt crabs, or cut sticks? Somehow, the whole band had to make up their minds, so they could act together.

Suppose their digging-sticks were dull. How did they decide what to do about it? Perhaps one of the band pointed toward the fiery mountain. Then he uttered a sound. And all understood, for the sound meant "Fire." It was a word!

Gradually, words were invented for foods, places, animals, and other things. After a very long time—perhaps a hundred thousand years—the creatures knew as many words as a three-year-old child knows today.

With these wonderful words, they could talk about themselves and their work. They talked about the sun and the rain, the moon and the stars. Words helped them to think. The more words they knew, the more things they could think about. And the more they thought, the more they had to say.

Over the centuries, a marvelous thing had happened.
In learning to speak and think and work together, the
creatures had become people. They were the first people
in the world.

The children of the first people had more to learn than any other young creatures that had ever lived.

Have you ever watched a baby animal to see how it learns? It imitates its mother. A kitten plays at being a cat. It's a copy-cat. It sees its mother catch a mouse. The kitten tries. Soon it, too, can catch a mouse.

Human babies have to learn harder things than that. They have to learn what words mean, and how to talk. They hear grown-ups and older children talking. They try, too. They repeat one word, then another.

While babies are trying to talk, their brains grow. Because this takes time, children develop slowly. Meanwhile, they need the care of grown-ups. When they begin to talk and understand, they learn many things from the grown-ups.

So it was with the first children. They learned to speak and understand. Then they learned how to watch for enemies, how to gather food, how to make a digging-stick, how to look for fire. There was so much to learn!

The first children went wherever the grown-ups went. Sometimes the band went on a treasure hunt, and the children tagged along.

Imagine such a trip. A band of people are walking along a riverbank. Sometimes a boy or a girl lifts a stone and finds a salamander. All at once, the children listen. What is that roaring sound? The sound grows louder as they go up the trail. They see a rainbow arching over the stream. A cliff towers into the sky, and from the cliff-top pours a flood of spray.

Near the waterfall, the people come to a gravel beach. The children don't mind the stones—this is a treasure hunt. Every now and then someone bends down and picks up a gleaming pebble. It is a flint—a lump of hard mineral from the cliff.

After they have gathered a number of flints, the people go to a camping-place by the river. There the men and boys squat in a circle. Each takes a flint and begins to hammer it with a stone. He strikes off chips until one side is flat. Then, carefully, he aims a blow at the flint. A large flake cracks away. Thin and sharp along one edge, it will make a good blade. It can be used for trimming a stick.

Wherever they go, the people watch the trail ahead. Perhaps they will meet some other band.

As they walk along, this may happen. One of the men will point ahead, and all stop to look. They see a group coming up the trail. Who, or what, are those creatures? It is wise to be careful. Some of the men and women take pieces of food and hold them high, so they can be seen. The strangers do the same.

One of the men calls out, "We are people of the river." A voice from the other band replies, "We are people of the woods." Then the bands meet and share the food of friendship.

There came a time when the rains failed, and streams dried up. Plants died. Grubs, crayfish, frogs, and all the other little food animals disappeared. Many bands of people starved. Others wandered away.

Some of the wanderers traveled on and on. At last they came to a strange, treeless land. They had never seen a country like this. The ground was flat. It stretched so far, it seemed to meet the sky. And grass grew everywhere. This new land was the plain.

The wanderers kept alive by hunting lizards and ground squirrels. Often they saw herds of antelope, horses, and other hoofed animals feeding on the grass. When they tried to get near the herds, the animals would dash away.

One day the wanderers came upon a band of strange people who were carrying long, straight sticks. They heard the strangers call out in an unknown language. The wanderers said, "These creatures do not speak as we do. But they do speak. They are people!"

The bands watched each other for a while. Then they came nearer, holding out pieces of food. The men of each band saw that the others had different kinds of flint tools. They examined one another's flints, and exchanged a few. In this way, each band learned how to use new tools.

How did people manage to live on the wide, grassy plain? This was a land for the swift and the strong. The grazing beasts were swift. They could run from danger. The hunting beasts were strong. Compared with such creatures, people were slow and weak. But they had gifts greater than strength and swiftness. They had good brains and skillful hands, and they had learned how to work together.

In the course of time, the people of the plain invented many useful things. They took flint pebbles and chipped them, shaping them into tools. From flint, they made choppers, scrapers, and knives. Then they thought of a marvelous weapon. They made a sharp flint point, and tied it to the end of a stick. Thus they invented the spear. This weapon, when thrown straight and true, would kill the biggest game.

Armed with spears, the people trailed the hoofed animals. They hid at watering-places and speared the beasts when they came to drink.

Fire was needed to cook the flesh of the hoofed animals. So the people kept a campfire burning all the time. When they moved to a new place, they would light a torch and carry the fire with them. Where the fire was, that place was home.

What if the fire should go out? Then the people would have no home. Without fire, the camp would be cold, the night dark. What would the people do? Where could they get a new fire? They could go off searching for some band that had fire. But before they found one, a long time might pass. And the people would be cold and hungry.

For thousands of years, fire was like a wild thing that had to be hunted. Then, at last, fire was tamed by man. How did it happen? Perhaps some hunter made a discovery while working on a spear. He rubbed pieces of wood together, and noticed that the rubbing made them hot. This gave him an idea. He began to scrape the point of a stick against a piece of wood. He scraped and scraped. Loose bits of the wood began to smoke. Then—out of the wood sprang a flame! Fire was tamed! Now people could make fire whenever they wished.

When animals saw a campfire, they knew that hunting people were there. The lions knew. The wild dogs knew. The dogs would creep up. They would come around the fire.

The dogs had always followed great hunters. When lions were hunting, dogs trailed after them, hoping to feed on the lions' leftovers. When men became hunters, the dogs began to follow the men. They would gather around a kill, and watch the hunters cut up the carcass. The dogs knew that some parts would be left for them.

At night, while people slept around their fire, dogs lay nearby, just beyond the circle of light. Their eyes gleamed in the dark. They watched the man on guard, and he watched them. Once in a while he tossed a stone, to keep them away from the sleeping children. Sometimes he tossed a bone. Then the crunching of teeth was heard.

Hunters welcomed the dogs around their camp. When they were there, no enemy could sneak up. If lions came, the dogs howled. The men awakened, and took up spears and firebrands to keep the lions away.

For thousands of years, hunters followed the hoofed animals. Some wandered far to the North, and reached a land where winter storms covered the plain with snow. Here lived the reindeer, the musk ox, the woolly mammoth, the woolly rhinoceros. All these creatures had thick fur to keep them warm.

The people had their campfire, but this was not
enough. They couldn't sit by the fire all the time. They
had to hunt. So they took the furry skins of animals, made
warm clothing, and covered themselves from head to foot.

At night, the band took refuge in a cave. When
gales howled in the dark world outside, the people sat
around their fire, feasting and singing.

Certain hunters roamed a country of green hills, where sheep grazed. These people trailed a flock of sheep just as people in the North followed reindeer. Often wolves attacked the sheep, frightening the flock away. So the people made war on the wolves.

Hunters were careful not to scare the flock they followed. When they needed meat, they looked for a sheep straying by itself. Sometimes they coaxed an animal away from the flock. They would take a lambskin and stuff it so that it looked like a lamb. Hiding behind a bush, they held up the dummy lamb. Soon a sheep at the edge of the flock would come over to investigate.

Someone had this idea: why not try to use a real, live lamb? The hunters caught some lambs and tied them near the camp. The lambs grew tame. The wild sheep often gathered near them. In time, the sheep got used to the people, and the people began to herd them. Perhaps that was how hunters became the first shepherds.

Among the people of every land, men and boys did one kind of work, and women and girls did another. Men hunted game. Women gathered plants.

Women of the forest knew where to find many kinds of fruit, seeds, and roots. They waited for each kind of plant to ripen. When the time came, the women slung the babies on their backs, called the girls, and went to gather the crop.

Part of the food was eaten right away, and part was saved. Then, if hunters found no game, the people did not go hungry. They had the women's harvest of plants.

After meals, scraps were thrown on a garbage heap. Sometimes there were seeds among the scraps, and a few of them sprouted. But before the shoots grew up, the people moved their camp to some other place where hunting was better.

Perhaps, when a group of women were searching for food, they came to an old camping-place. And there they made a discovery. Around the old garbage heap, a garden grew.

From that time, women planted gardens, and people stayed at their camp long enough to reap the harvest. When they moved to a new place, the first thing they did was to burn away the trees and scrub, and clear the ground for a garden.

On the plain, hunters moved too often to have gardens, but the women did gather a certain wild food. This food came from grass. After the grass had flowered, seeds ripened in ears on the stems. The women cut and gathered the stems, and beat them to thresh out the seeds. Those seeds were the first cereal grains.

Time passed, and the climate changed. Less and less rain fell. Grass died out, and the land became desert. Only a few of the hoofed animals managed to stay alive. They gathered along the banks of streams flowing from the hills. There the animals found water and grass.

The people, too, lived by the streams, hunting the animals there. At certain times of the year, the streams overflowed their banks. When this happened, the women scattered seeds over the wet earth. They always used the best seeds, so the grain improved. Finally, one kind of grass became wheat, and another kind became barley.

After the harvest, the straw was left in the field. Sheep and cattle came to eat it. The people began to herd the beasts, and finally tamed them. Thus began a wonderful way of living. By raising both grain and animals, the people had plenty of food.   Many families could settle in one place, where they built a village.   They learned how to make pots of clay, how to weave cloth, and how to work metals.   And they taught these skills to their children.

Today we follow in the path of all the people who have lived before us. We work and learn together, and together we discover new wonders of the world.